ANTHONY ROBINSON writes children's books and teaches.
He has lived and travelled all over the world, from his original home
in Australia to Asia, Southeast Asia and Europe, and now lives in Cambridge.
He is keen to give a voice to the voiceless, be they refugees who have fled
their own countries, children living normal lives in vastly different cultures,
or children living in difficult circumstances.

ANNEMARIE YOUNG writes books for children and works
with educational publishers. She has lived and travelled all over the world,
and now lives in Cambridge. She has worked with over 100 children's authors
and illustrators from all corners of the globe. She loves the whole process
of publishing, and still finds it exciting to open the first copy
of one of the books she has written or worked on.

JUNE ALLAN can't remember a time when she didn't love drawing.
Her mum says she used to sit and draw in her pram!
After twenty years as a professional portrait painter, June illustrated
her first book in 1999 and since then has illustrated many children's books.
June lives in Edinburgh with her husband and two children,
Fern the guinea pig, and lots of goldfish.

This book is dedicated to Mohammed and Susan,
and to all those who are struggling to be free.

The authors would like to thank the Medical Foundation
for the Care of Victims of Torture for their help,
and for introducing them to Mohammed and Susan.

MOHAMMED'S JOURNEY

A Refugee Diary

Anthony Robinson

and

Annemarie Young

Illustrated by June Allan

F

FRANCES LINCCLN
CHILDREN'S BOOKS

This is Mohammed's own story. We follow him on a journey from his family home in Kirkuk, Iraq. He travels by bus, on horseback, in an inflatable raft on a raging river and finally, hiding in a lorry on a ship. This journey takes him from Kirkuk to the Iraq-Iran border, through Iran, into Turkey and then on to England and safety.

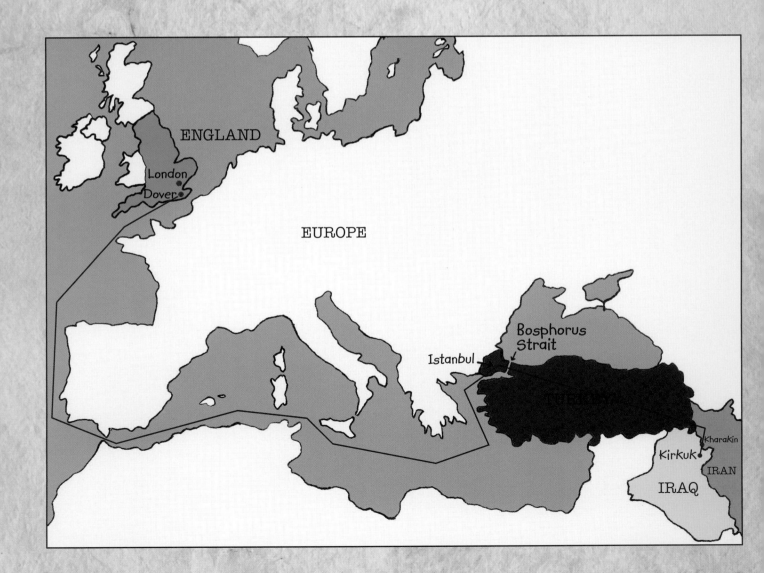

My name is Mohammed. I was born in 1994 in Kirkuk, a city in the north of Iraq. My family is Kurdish. I lived with my mum and dad. We had a happy life together. My mum was a cashier and my dad was a taxi driver.

Things started to go wrong for our family before I was born, way back in 1991. My mum's brother was killed by Ali Hassan, a relative of Saddam Hussein, the leader of Iraq at that time. He was killed outside our door. Shot. Along with 40 other people. Trouble came into our family then. Like a dark thing, my mum says.

But the real trouble started for us in 1994, just before I was born.

The beginning of the end – Kirkuk, 1994

My dad, along with many other Kurds, was secretly working for a group in opposition to Saddam. A lot of people were doing this – these opposition groups were our only voice. Saddam hated the Kurds and gave us a lot of trouble. That's why, in 1994, when Mum was pregnant with me, the soldiers came for the first time. That was the beginning of the end for our family. We were scared all the time after that.

They took Dad away for six months and Mum for 40 days.
And they also later took Mum away twice for interrogation.
It was hard because she was pregnant with me, and Dad
was in prison. Mum was working as a nurse at that time too.
There was a war with Iran, and everybody had to help out.

Kirkuk – 1994-2000

Even though we were scared, life went on as normal. I played with my friends and cousins. We played a lot outside – football and with toy cars. I wasn't at school. You don't start before the age of six in Iraq. All my friends and some of my family lived on the same street. We all played together. And all the houses were the same too. Single storey. None of them had stairs. That's one thing that's strange in England. Up and down. I always have to remember what I need when I come downstairs because otherwise I spend all day going up and down. It's funny.

Anyway, in those days my mum worked and I would go to my grandmother's or Mum's sister's while she was at work. Dad's sister also had kids and we would spend time with them too. It was nice. Nice and normal.

Time to flee – Kirkuk, 2000

Then it happened again, in October 2000. The soldiers from Saddam came, three of them, with guns, and beat us all, especially my dad, and they took him away. They beat me on the shoulder with their rifle butts. It still hurts.

We haven't seen my dad since then. Nobody has. My mum's sister heard he is dead, but we don't know for sure. I will never forget that time. Never. Seeing my mum and dad beaten like that. It stays in front of my eyes. I used to draw pictures of that ... the last time I saw my dad. It makes me afraid and angry.

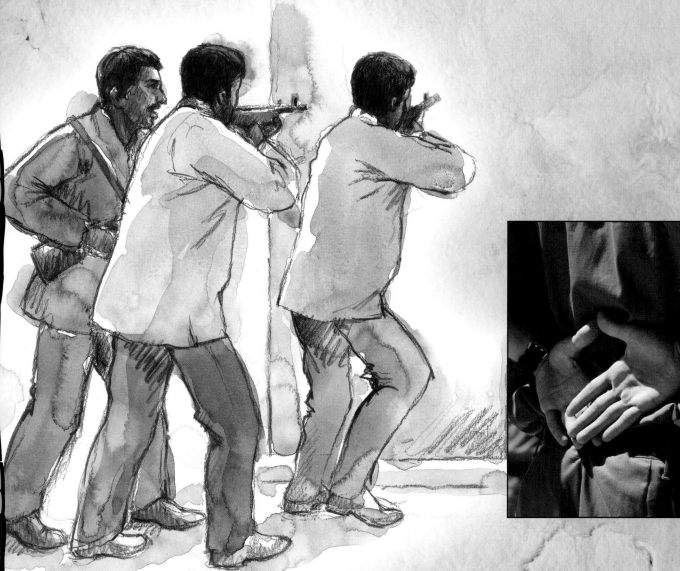

I'm still afraid really, because, as they were taking my dad away, one of the soldiers turned to us and said, "We'll be coming back for you." I can still see and hear them.

After the soldiers had gone, Mum said, "We're leaving." She was sure they would come back for us.

We left two days later.

Leaving Kirkuk – Iraq-Iran Border, 2000

Mum got a few things together, not much, and we went to our uncle's house in Kharakin on the Iraq-Iran border. We travelled in a sort of taxi with another family. It took two hours and I cried a couple of times because I was hungry. I felt really angry too. I just couldn't understand how someone could break into your house, beat you, and then take away someone from your family.

It was all in such a quickly, quickly rush.

We stayed with my uncle overnight, and the next day, before sunrise, we left Kharakin and walked for two hours to the Iraqi border checkpoint. We found the bus we were looking for. It was a seven-seater and there were 20 of us all squashed in. It was so crowded on the bus that we couldn't take anything with us – only the clothes we had on, and Mum had some papers. That's all. I cried then, because I couldn't take the train my dad had given me.

The driver gave me some biscuits. He was kind.

Into Iran - 2000

We went round the Iraqi checkpoint in the bus, to avoid the guards. Then we had to get out of the bus before the Iranian checkpoint, and go round it on foot. It took three hours before we found our bus again. There was lots of confusion. Then the bus drove for four hours into Iran. After that, we crossed a small river in a small boat. There were five of us and we had to row or paddle. My mum lost all her papers then, because the water was so fast and dangerous. Her bag with the papers just got swept away.

Then we came to another checkpoint, still in Iran, and crossed in a safe place, on horses. This took about 20 minutes. I was on a horse with the man who was taking us to a house where we stayed for the night. I think that's the first time Mum gave me sleeping pills. I couldn't make a noise. It would've been too dangerous.

We stayed in this house for one night. We had wonderful Iranian rice and stuff. We were so hungry. We left on a bus the next day before dawn, with lots of other fleeing Iraqis This bus took us to a village in Turkey. The journey took two days and we only stopped at night for the toilet. I remember the darkness.

On our way – Turkey, 2000

We stayed in the Turkish village for two nights. We had to wait for a man to arrange a place on a boat to cross the Bosphorus. We were finally put into lorries, with four or five other people. This was late October, and very cold and wet. The top of the lorry was all ripped so we got wet. I remember it was always dark in the lorry. Too dark to see. It was dangerous too. The floor of the lorry was covered in bits of metal and broken bricks. We were always hurting ourselves. Cold, afraid, wet, and always hungry.

We didn't really know what was happening to us most of the time.

The lorry took us to Istanbul, where we stayed for a few days in a flat with other Iraqi people. Then the lorry was driven onto the boat. We didn't know where we would stop. We had no food and only a little water. We had to use an empty bottle for the toilet. I think we spent six or seven days without food. I was so hungry I felt sick all the time.

The boat stopped twice. We didn't know where. We could see stars, that's all, and it was freezing. It was always dark in the lorry. We didn't know if it was day or night. It was just dark.

Arrival in England – Dover, 2000

We finally stopped in the UK port of Dover. I banged on the side
of the lorry with a stone to let the driver know we were there.
I had been given some stones for this and told this was my job.
The driver came round and opened the lorry, saw us, closed up
the lorry again and went away. We didn't know what was happening.
We were cold, dirty, hungry and afraid.

Then after about two hours, the police came.

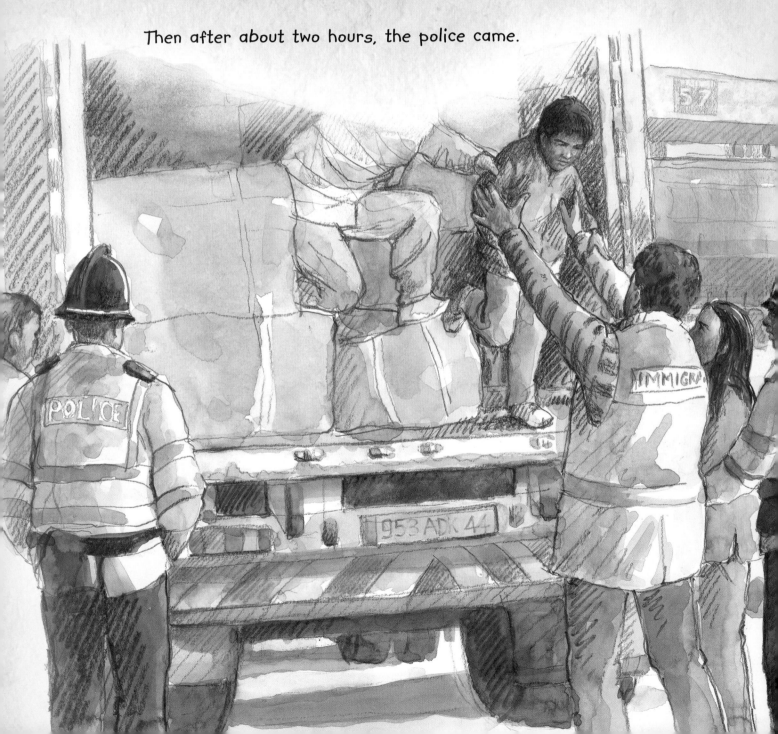

The police were kind. They took us to an interview room and gave us sandwiches and drinks. It was so wonderful to eat and be warm. And no more darkness. I was so excited I ran to the toilets and washed my face.

A Kurdish interpreter came and then we were taken to a hotel nearby, where we stayed for 35 days. That was all of November. I slept in a normal bed and had a TV. When I woke up there were lots of other children there too. It was wonderful to stop. To stay somewhere.

Settling in – Dover, 2000

I remember my first breakfast in England – toast and jam.
Boy, I was hungry. Then fish and chips and burgers and chips.
We still only had the clothes we had arrived in. Then a charity
gave us clothes, books and toys. It was just great to be with
other people. Safe and not so afraid. I played in a park with
other children and walked around Dover.

The Kurdish family we had left Kirkuk with were still with us, but
they went to Hull after two weeks. There were other Kurdish
people around too, which was good for me because
it's my language. Mum speaks Arabic too, but I can't.

Playing football in the park

Mum got really sick three days after we arrived. She couldn't even open her eyes for two days, but the Kurdish family looked after us. I never saw her much when she was sick.

A new beginning – London, 2000-2002

When Mum got better we went to Immigration for an interview. Aaron, our caseworker, helped us. He got us into the Medical Foundation so we could get counselling.

In January 2001, we moved to the Pembury Hotel in Stamford Hill. One time I got really sick and had to go to hospital. I had a very high temperature, felt dizzy and couldn't see clearly. But I got better after a few days.

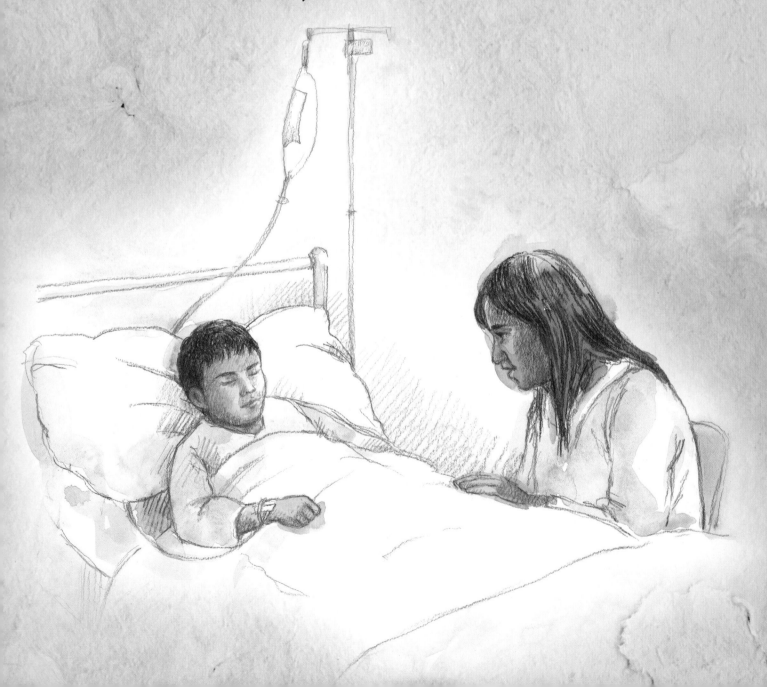

In July 2001, we moved to a flat. We stayed there for a year. We got leave to stay in the UK in 2002. It was fantastic. We felt so relieved. I was really glad for my mum because she met Fuad, another Iraqi Kurd refugee. He's my stepdad now, but he's still waiting for leave to stay, so Mum's a bit worried. I started at Pools Park Primary School in September 2002. Then in October, my little sister Sara was born. It was a nice time for us. I hope Sara's dad can stay. I just wish my dad was here.

I liked school. My mum helped me and I also got extra English lessons, but mostly I've learned English from other kids at school, and from TV. I liked Pools Park because there were lots of other kids like me – from Kosovo, Albania, Iraq and even Africa, as well as lots of English kids.

My little sister and me

Life now

I'm at high school now. The Islington Arts and Media School.
I'm doing well and I really like it. I also really like the house
where we live. We moved here in October 2004. It's only
temporary, but I like it here and I want to stay.

The past is still in front of my eyes. I see a counsellor and go
to the Wednesday Group at the Medical Foundation. I like that.
There are other kids there who have problems too. Not exactly
like mine, but similar. They are from all over the world.
We just talk about our week and stuff. It helps. We do
plays and poems. It's great.

Sometimes we go to the sea at Southend or galleries. I love the seaside. I like the space. It's calm and it's fun. I also have some Polish friends and we go swimming sometimes. I play football too. I used to be the goalie, but now I'm a forward. I prefer that. It's an important position, more attacking, and I'm good.

I like almost everything here. But I have bad dreams and sometimes feel scared. I still can't forget what happened in Kirkuk ... what happened to my dad. For the first two years in England I kept drawing pictures of when they beat us and took my dad away. I've stopped that now, but I still get afraid sometimes, especially if I see a policeman. I hide.

I have a stepdad now and that's good, but he's not my real dad is he? I miss my dad.

Me and my sister now

Towards my future

I try not to think of Kirkuk, but the memories just come. Often when I least expect them, and all mixed up. Good, bad, horrible, being afraid, playing football in my street, my dad. Mum still has some contact with her mum. Grandma is sick – she has had two heart attacks and has asthma. She's not really old, but she's been sick since her son was killed in front of her in 1991.

I can think about the future now. I couldn't for a long time. I have friends, a nice school and my mum seems happier. And I have a sister. I feel safer, especially now we know we can stay. I know Mum does too.

My mum, my little sister and me

Someday I want to be a pilot. But I know that I have to do well at school. No school means no job to me. And no job means no future. I like my school subjects, especially PE and ICT. I really enjoy PC games and have some good ones that I've downloaded. I'm saving now for a PlayStation - that's the next thing for me. And I intend to work hard at school. I want a good life, but most of all I want what I can't have. I want my dad back.

Did you know?

★ The Republic of Iraq is a country of 169,000 square kilometres (106,000 square miles) and a population of about 22 million people. The two main rivers, the Euphrates and the Tigris, have run through over 5,000 years of Iraqi history.

★ Iraq has borders with Turkey to the north, Iran to the east, the Persian Gulf to the south-east, Kuwait and Saudi Arabia to the south and Jordan and Syria to the west.

★ Kirkuk, with a population of 800,000 people, is an important oil city in the north of Iraq. It is the capital of At Ta'mim Province. It is 250 kilometres (156 miles) north of Baghdad, Iraq's capital city, and close to Iran in the east; Turkey is to the north.

★ The Kirkuk oilfields were opened in 1934 by the Iraq Petroleum Company. They have remained an important source of oil and trouble ever since.

★ The people speak Kurdish, Arabic, Assyrian, Turkmen and Armenian.

What happened?

The recent history of Iraq, and therefore Kirkuk, is very troubled and brutal, and this is just a brief outline.

This period is really the history of one man: Saddam Hussein.

Saddam plotted and murdered his way to power, and in July 1979, finally became President of Iraq. In 1980 he attacked Iraq's nearest neighbor, Iran. The war, which Iraq lost, cost millions of lives and lasted until 1988. During this period the Iraqi Kurds were also sprayed with poisonous chemicals, killing thousands of men, women and children.

In 1990 Saddam's army attacked Kuwait, another near neighbour. Iraq also lost this short war, in which the United States and combined Arab forces drove Iraq from Kuwait.

Throughout this time, Saddam and his political friends worked to hold onto power inside Iraq. As a result, many people were arrested, tortured and executed. Many just disappeared.

The end finally came in early 2003 when US and British forces attacked Iraq. The war itself was over very quickly. Saddam was captured near his hometown of Tikrit and tried before an Iraqi court. He was executed on 30 December 2006.

All through this period, it was the Iraqi people who suffered. And they continue to suffer. Since the last war ended, over 100,000 Iraqi men, women and children have been killed, as different groups try to win control of the country. The US has lost 4,000 soldiers and over two million Iraqis have been displaced.

MOHAMMED'S JOURNEY copyright © Frances Lincoln Limited 2009
Text copyright © Anthony Robinson and Annemarie Young 2009
Illustrations copyright © June Allan 2009

First published in Great Britain and the USA in 2009 by
Frances Lincoln Children's Books, 4 Torriano Mews,
Torriano Avenue, London NW5 2RZ

www.franceslincoln.com

First paperback published in Great Britain and the USA in 2011

A catalogue record for this book is available from the British Library.

ISBN 978-1-84780-209-5

Illustrated with watercolour

Printed in Dongguan, Guangdong, China by Toppan Leefung in December, 2010

1 3 5 7 9 8 6 4 2

MORE TITLES IN THE REFUGEE DIARY SERIES FROM FRANCES LINCOLN CHILDREN'S BOOKS

Hamzat's Journey
Anthony Robinson
Illustrated by June Allan

Hamzat grew up in Chechnya at a time of war. It was hard for his whole family. They were always hungry, afraid, and in winter, very cold. But one day, on his way to school, Hamzat's life changed forever. He stepped on a landmine and lost his right leg below the knee. With the help of his family and others, Hamzat eventually reached England, to get a new leg and start a new life.
The story tells of how a boy and his family overcame the great difficulties of war.

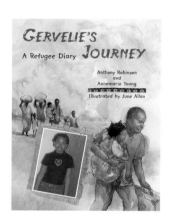

Gervelie's Journey
Anthony Robinson and Annemarie Young
Illustrated by June Allan

Gervelie was born in the Republic of Congo. When fighting broke out in her home city of Brazzaville, her family had to flee to safety. Her father became a wanted man and was forced into hiding. The family was torn apart forever.
Gervelie and her father escaped the country and travelled to the UK to seek asylum.

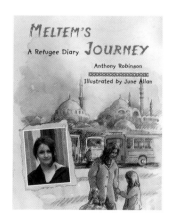

Meltem's Journey
Anthony Robinson
Illustrated by June Allan

Meltem is a Kurdish girl who grew up on a farm in a village in eastern Turkey. It was a happy time until the day Turkish soldiers came to the village. The family's life changed forever. Meltem's father fled to Germany. The family joined him and they all later travelled to England where they experienced racial discrimination, and spent several months in a detention centre, awaiting deportation. However, with support from the Children's Commissioner and their own strength and resilience, they prevailed, and were eventually granted asylum.

Frances Lincoln titles are available from all good bookshops.
You can also buy books and find out more about your favourite titles, authors and illustrators on our website: www.franceslincoln.com